How To

And Outsmart Anyone

Time Tested Strategies That Will Give You the Upper Hand When Dealing With People

By Landon T. Smith

Table of Contents

Introduction

We live in a world where a quick tongue, a sharp mind and fast reflexes can get you very far. We live in a world full of people who are ready to insult, take advantage of or otherwise defeat us in verbal combat, so it pays to be on your toes of all time. But what if you're not someone who's particularly well versed in learning how to turn a conversation on its head, or how to defend yourself well in an argument, it can be difficult to navigate through life. But don't worry, because that's why we're here! With this book, you're going to learn all of the valuable ways to handle people, be it your boss who won't get off your case, a nagging spouse or a sleazy car salesman. We're going to learn the underlying psychological principles of persuasion, verbal self-defense and negotiation, so that you can handle any situation dealing with people with ease and skill. If you've always wanted to know how to get the upper hand when it comes to dealing with the human element, learn the reason why people tend to get emotional during any kind of discussion and be able to overcome just about any kind of interpersonal obstacle, then this is the book for you!

We're going to cover three major areas of learning how to outmaneuver your opponents. The first section will be about the art of active listening and evaluation, the second section will be about how people convey emotions through works and body language and the third and final section will be a list of tried and true tactics that work in any area of interpersonal conflict. Are you ready? Let's begin.

Chapter 1: What's Really Going On?

The situation is a classic one. A husband and wife are arguing vehemently about something minor, perhaps it's about finding the right restaurant to eat at for the evening, or maybe it's about someone not living up to an agreement, such as the husband having forgotten to get the mail or take out the trash. Imagine that you are an outsider, watching these two hurl insults and shouts at one another. Indeed, when we are not a part of the argument, when we aren't emotionally invested in the situation, it can seem incredibly strange to witness two grown adults violently arguing over seemingly insignificant things. Is the trash really that important? So much so that a woman is willing to scream until her face is red? Is defending the fact that he forgot worth more than his marriage? To an outsider, we would shake our heads and wonder why they don't just talk about their differences. Yet, that is because we are entirely removed from the situation. Imagine, for a moment that you are inside the head of the woman. Her husband didn't take out the trash, as she had asked time and time again. What's going through her mind at that moment? What is contributing to her intense anger? Why does she care so much about the trash?

Handling and resolving conflict, believe it or not, isn't about winning through brute force or domination. It's not about being able to effectively cow your opponent into submission or tricking someone into making a crucial misstep. Conflict resolution isn't like wrestling, you don't get to make a clever move that will suddenly win you the match. Unlike a physical fight, where the goal is to beat up your opponent, in conflict resolution, the goal is to win completely and the only way you can win is for both parties to be satisfied with the arrangement.

Put yourself in either the husband or wife's shoes in that moment. Consider what they would ultimately want to see. Would the husband want to completely defeat his wife, forcing her into submission and dealing damage to her ego and self-esteem? Is that the ideal scenario? Not at all! Would the wife truly want her husband to be a battered and broken man, compliant with her demands and unable to stand up for himself? No. So why do they fight so loudly and angrily? Because they both want something for themselves. They both want satisfaction. The real question isn't "why are they fighting?" the real question is "what do they want?"

As you watch this argument unfold, you must ask yourself what you think these two want. At a glance, from the words being hurled, we can imagine that the desires are relatively simple. The wife wants the trash taken out and to be apologized to and the husband doesn't want to admit that he was wrong. It's very clear by the words they speak that this is what both of them want. But, as you're going to learn, the first crucial lesson of learning how to maneuver and move through conflict is to evaluate what's going on beneath the surface level.

People are complex beings. They are, at all times, filled with half a dozen conflicting thoughts, ideas and beliefs that tend to skew the way they perceive reality. While we like to believe that the world works in objective absolute truths, the reality is that people are intensely subjective. They are biased and skewed, when confronted with contradicting evidence, they usually tend to warp the evidence to agree with their beliefs instead of changing them. People process events through a lens, a filter that warps reality to agree with their ideas. The best way to be able to deal with people isn't to overpower them through clever phrases or brilliant tactics, rather the best way is to focus on the motivations behind their actions. This can be tricky because understanding human motivation requires a certain level of insight. It requires the ability to look deeper and consider what the person is thinking. It essentially requires empathy.

Consider the fighting couple again. The wife is screaming and angry. Why? Because there is something in her belief structure that is provoking a great anger inside of her. Does she feel belittled by her husband's refusal to do her bidding? Is she a control freak who needs to be in control in order to feel safe? Was she raised to believe that a wife should be pampered at all costs? These questions cannot be quickly answered, as they require a greater insight into the human mind, but these questions must be raised when looking at a situation. Likewise, when we see the vitriol that the husband slings back, we must ask why does he act that way? Does he believe that a man should never be questioned? Does he feel hurt and scared by his partner and is lashing out of a desire to protect himself?

People are rarely healthy and pretty on the inside. They are fiercely self-protective and if they feel threatened will adopt a variety of patterns that are meant to protect themselves. We'll talk more about self-protection in the next section, but just for now take notice that when conflict arises and emotions get out of control, it is because both parties are feeling threatened on some level.

And so, we watch this argument come to a climax with the wife finally breaking down sobbing and the husband angrily storming out of the house. The entire thing started because she made a comment about the trash and he took it poorly. The question must be raised: was the whole thing really about the trash? Absolutely not. The first rule in understanding how to maneuver and outsmart your opponents is that you must always be willing to look beneath the surface of your opponent. You must be willing to listen to what they are saying, yes, but most importantly you must be able to see what is going on in their heads. You must see the subconscious elements that affect how we react to things and you can only achieve that by learning to listen to not only what a person is saying, but *how* a person is saying their words.

Consider how the argument might have gone between the husband and wife had the husband been able to listen to how his wife was speaking. She might have started with a very sharp barb like "Looks like someone forgot to take the trash out again. Can't you do anything right just for once?" Of course, he's going to experience a deep sense of frustration and anger at those words, provided that he only looks at the surface of those words. Yes, they are incendiary and inflammatory – on the surface. But what does she actually mean by that? The art of learning to look beneath involves making the conscious decision to step away from taking things personal and instead looking at the challenge before you. The challenge at the very beginning of a conflict isn't to overcome the person, the challenge is to actually understand the person. If you don't understand the person, then you won't be able to solve the problem, if anything you'll just be able to temporarily make it go away. Solving the problem in conflict is actually best for all parties involved. It's, in fact, the only way to truly win. Outsmarting a person isn't about dominating, it's about getting the best possible results.

So, imagine that the husband listens to the words and resists the urge to take them personally. Instead of seeking dominance and defensiveness, he begins instead to seek understanding. In the process of seeking understanding, he takes a moment to evaluate what his wife actually wants. He sees that she wants him to take out the trash, but then he considers her feelings on a deeper level. He considers the fact that she feels hurt by his actions. Her anger, he reasons, is a product of a feeling of neglect. She is hurling insults at him because she *feels* as if he doesn't care. He identifies that the conflict has nothing to do with the trash itself, but rather with how she *feels* about him neglecting the trash. He might even ask a few questions, such as "why do you feel like I can't do anything right?" or "you probably don't feel good when I don't take out the trash, huh?" In short, if he begins to seek understanding of the situation, it puts him in the higher position immediately.

If we look at the power dynamics of an argument, we must face the fact that there are also positions. Someone who has the upper hand will win, so we must ask the question: what is the upper hand? Is the upper hand being able to pound someone into the ground? Not at all! Is having the upper hand meaning you are inflicting grievous wounds upon your opponent in an emotional way? No! Having the upper hand means that you are positioned to have the maximum advantage in the conversation. Understanding, in mechanical terms, brings you the biggest advantage because you are able to understand what's actually going on. It allows you to understand the rules of the game a little better.

What's the difference between Chess and Checkers? Quite a lot. There are many different rules and you would play Chess very differently than you would play checkers. But they both have the same board. Imagine how much of a disaster it would be if you were to try and play checkers when the actual game was chess. If you don't have understanding, you might not be actually having the same argument. Imagine if the husband didn't realize at all that his wife was angry about feeling neglected and instead was trying to simply validate his position. Without understanding, why would he ever feel the need to apologize? After all, he wasn't trying to intentionally forget the trash. He wasn't trying to spite her, nor was he working to cause her harm. He forgot, people forget things all the time, in fact she locked herself out of the house just last week. So, he gets caught up into the discussion about the trash and tries to argue against her on those merits. He doesn't have understanding and he might as well be trying to play checkers against a Chess master.

So, as you begin to learn how to get the upper hand in conflict resolution, negotiation and handling aggressive people, you must seek understanding above all else. When you desire to understand your opponent's position, it will allow you to move onto the next steps. So how do we increase our understanding of our opponent? Well, let's look at a few steps below.

Understanding Tip 1: Resist the Pull

The fastest way to lose an argument is to get pulled into what your opponent wants to talk about. Why is that? It's because they are entirely colored by their own perceptions. When you get pulled into the argument on their terms, it means that you are working with their thoughts, ideas and definitions. The Pull is a term we'll use to explain that emotional desire to jump into the discussion without seeking understanding. The Pull happens as a knee jerk reaction, usually to some kind of insult or situation. When a person angrily shouts at you, calls you names, or you're taken by surprise by something such as a demotion or you're suddenly in a conflict that you didn't realize was coming, you can be tempted to engage without knowing what you're going to be doing. The Pull seeks to drag you into conflict without preparation.

You must, at all costs, avoid The Pull. This isn't particularly easy at first because we are primarily emotional creatures. We tend not to realize just how strong our emotions can influence us until we start learning how to resist our initial reactions to situations. Your emotional reaction may vary depending on the situation. We might end up angry, afraid, worried, confused or a combination of those feelings, it depends on our temperaments and what is happening. What's important is that we don't confuse our *feelings* with truth. How you feel about something has nothing to do with reality. But this is what The Pull tries to do. The Pull tries to convince us that what we are feeling is true. If you feel threatened, you'll want to defend yourself. If you're feeling worthless, you might be convinced to do something that you really don't want to do. We are affected by The Pull whenever another person comes into some kind of conflict with us. It could be something as simple as a negotiation or something as intense as being served divorce papers. The action that triggers the emotional surge doesn't matter, but our reaction does.

So, what do we do instead of giving into The Pull? What do we do instead of giving into our intense emotions in the moment? We must come to recognize that our feelings have no impact on reality and that until we have a full understanding of the situation, we cannot truly be victorious. Feelings can be deceptive. They don't convey truth, they just convey what you believe in the moment. But initial reactions rarely have full understanding of what's going on. Adopt a rule of never immediately responding to conflict when it pops up. It might seem counterintuitive at first, but outmaneuvering your opponent first requires you to know what is needed to win. Overreacting or misjudging what the situation is will just end up getting you into trouble or worse, will cause you to lose in the conflict. We lose a conflict whenever we are unable to achieve the ideal circumstance.

Understand Tip 2: Step Out

Everyone is the hero in their own movie. No one, and I mean no one, considers themselves to be the bad guy. Sure, some people might acknowledge that they're rude, or mean or condescending, but deep down, just about everyone believes that they are the protagonist in their own story. This is no different in conflict. Conflict arises because two people disagree about a situation. Disagreements only occur when both parties believe they are right, but those beliefs conflict. So, that means no one on the other side of the table believes that they are the bad guy. This is important to know, because as you learn how to seek understanding of any given situation, you must be able to step out of your own perspective and step into theirs.

You are the good guy, of course. There's nothing wrong with that because we are all the heroes in our own story. So, everything that you do, on some subconscious level, is justifiable because you are the good guy. At least that's how our minds think. Once again, this is just how we are as people. So since just about everything you do can be justified, wouldn't it make sense that your opponent would believe the same? It can be so incredibly easy to vilify or demonize your opponent, you can easily say "my boss is just a thug," or "my ex-husband is a psycho," but the reality is that these people have complex beliefs and motivations that have led them to acting the way that they do. And they believe, on some level, that they are justified in their actions.

This means that if you are going to have a better understanding of their mindsets, you must be able to step out of your own shoes and instead learn to step into theirs. You've got to be able to think about their feelings, their emotions, beliefs and ideas. You've got to understand why they would act the way they do. If every action in their own mind is justified, then you must have an understanding of those justifications. This will enable you to communicate to them on a better level later on, and most importantly it will build up your empathy with them.

Empathy is the key to understanding your opponent. While it might not seem attractive, to learn how a person thinks and feels, it's probably one of the most powerful skills that you can learn. You see, when you know why a person feels the way they do, you have insight into how to resolve the conflict. Using the trash conflict again, when the husband understands why his wife is acting so harshly about something so minor, he has a better understanding of what he can do to resolve the conflict. Instead of just brazenly yelling about her, he could meet her on an emotional level, let her vent her feelings or listen to her without snapping to judgement. He could reaffirm her, talk to her, apologize to her and win the conflict by improving his relationship with her. He might not have been able to overcome her with fierce words that put her in her place, but he was able to increase the quality of their relationship. Which leads us to our next tip.

Understanding Tip 3: Value of Relationships

Outsmarting and outmaneuvering your opponent has tremendous value, but you must ask yourself what your objectives are. Do you desire to temporarily feel superior over someone? Do you desire to enjoy a short-lived victory that doesn't particularly serve you in the future? If your goal is to grind someone down into the dust, then you have a very limited view of how to win. A real victory isn't beating the crap out of someone and forcing them to admit that you are better than them. A real victory is improving your relationship with the person you are dealing with.

Now this might seem idealistic at first, but think about it for a moment. If the goal is always to improve the relationship, then the possibilities and benefits are absolutely endless. An improved relationship can positively affect your life and should always be sought after. After all, you catch more flies with honey than you do vinegar. If the goal is to just forcefully overcome your opponent, that's not really of the best benefit to you. The best benefit is to get another person to understand you sufficiently enough to desire a good outcome as well. Mutual agreement will always beat out submission any day of the week.

This means that if you are going to want to outsmart and outmaneuver your opponents, then your intentions must be, at the end of the day, to improve your relationship with them as you work to get your way. There's no reason you can't absolutely defeat an opposing salesman in a negotiation, but your desire shouldn't be to crush them. You must value relationships highly if you are going to achieve great things in discussion. A love for others will increase your capacity to have understanding. However, if you don't have a great love for your fellow man, then you will find that you won't be able to empathize or react properly when dealing with conflict. Your actions will be rough and brutish and while you might win a few battles you won't win the war.

Understanding Tip 4: Understand Yourself

Perhaps one of the most important things you must know as you are dealing with conflict is that if you don't have a solid understanding of yourself, you don't get very far. Many a man is able to spot his opponents weaknesses, but only a great one can look at their own weaknesses and realize that they are not perfect. When you acknowledge your feelings, your weaknesses, your shortcomings, you will have a far better chance of protecting yourself from situations that might take advantage of those weakness. For example, if you acknowledge that you have an anger problem and work on your temper continuously, you will do far better in a surprise situation, than if you were to refuse to acknowledge your own shortcomings.

Why do we as people tend to have trouble seeing our own flaws? Well, part of it is that we often fear that if we acknowledge something, it will become true. This is a silly type of reasoning, but many adults honestly believe that if they ignore some kind of flaw or shortcoming, their problems will go away. Instead of dealing with their issues head on, they develop some kind of willful ignorance, because they would rather be timid, or angry, or inflammatory rather than acknowledge that there is something that makes them weak. It might because they are afraid or because they are ignorant, but either way, if you don't handle your problems, your problems will manhandle you. You don't get stronger by learning to ignore your own personal issues, you get stronger by working through them. The more weaknesses that you know you have, the stronger that you are. If you look in the mirror and don't find anything wrong with you, it's not that you're perfect. It's that you don't have a realistic view of yourself.

When we understand our own weaknesses and fears, it expands our own understanding of our reactions. A heated exchange can be avoided if you realize the reason you are feeling so angry is because you are scared, or you can catch yourself before you make a crucial mistake that could potentially cause you to fall victim to The Pull. All of this will go into making you far more capable of understanding the conflict that is at hand.

So, there you have it, the first crucial step to winning a conflict: understanding what the actual conflict is about. So now that you know what the conflict is about, the question is raised: what's next? Well, let's go to step two: active listening.

Chapter 2: Do You Hear It?

The old joke goes, God gave us one mouth and two ears, so what does that tell you? We were meant to speak once and listen twice. While it might be a bit of a joke, it does have a solid principle behind it. In today's culture, we often feel an immense pressure to be the first to speak, to get our words out as quickly and aggressively as possible, as if there was some sort of timer in a conflict. If we don't get all of our words out in time, we can feel frustrated. When someone cuts us off, it feels unfair, or worse, if someone ignores what we had to say, we can feel entirely invalidated as a person. The desire to speak usually comes from the misplaced idea that speaking is more important than listening. But the reality is that listening is one of the most important parts of navigating conflict, because listening is how to identify what our opponent's goals are, what they are thinking and how we can best take advantage of that situation.

Do a quick evaluation of yourself: do you often find yourself waiting for the other person to finish talking so you can get a word in? Or do you listen to everything they say with intensity, focusing on not only the words they are using, but the other intangible things, such as body language, emotion and intonation? Oftentimes, if we aren't careful, we can default to the first category of thinking, just waiting to get our words out. When emotions rise and conflict intensifies, the desire to get the last word in can become even more intense. We lose focus on listening and think about winning.

Yet, the reality is that if you want to win, you've got to be able to listen. By focusing on what's going on, listening intently to what your opponent has to say, you will be far more informed than if you are busy thinking about what you are going to say next. Partly because since you haven't heard the full thing yet, you won't really know what to say next effectively anyway.

The discipline of listening intently to another person as they are talking, considering their words, picturing what they are saying and understanding them is known as Active Listening. It requires a certain level of concentration to be able to listen, absorb and recall exactly what the person has just said. Try a little experiment if you can, the next time you're talking to someone, try remembering everything that they just said to you. As the conversation unfolds, you might start to realize that it's not always that easy to recall what a person said, even if they just said it. If you aren't trained and disciplined in the art of active listening, you will find that it's not actually that easy to listen to each and every word another person says. Why is that? Well, quite simply because the mind is a very busy thing. It's trying to process information as quickly as it can and also supply you with the right things to say. If you are trying to respond as quickly as possible, you're going to be sacrificing your ability to recall. Instead, if you were to slow down and take each moment one step at a time, you'd find that active listening can vastly improve your reactions.

There are a couple of things that contribute to a good level of active listening. Let's take a look at each element.

Patience:

The brain is quick and tends to jump around. Sometimes, if you're quick on your feet, you might find that as a person is struggling to get an idea or sentence out, you already have an understanding of what they are saying. You might even be able to predict the words that are coming out of their mouth accurately. The temptation to be impatient and either finish their sentences or jump in and talk can be intense, but patience pays off in the long run. You never really know exactly how a person is going to deliver information and you might be missing out on some crucial nonverbal cues if all you're doing is waiting for your turn to jump in. Instead, try soaking in the moment and really take time to look at your opponent and learn what it is that they are saying. You might be surprised that the more engrossed you get into the situation, the easier it is to be patient with them.

Care:

Another element of active listening is that you need to care and have consideration for them. The more you care about a person, the more apt you are to listen to them. Just because you are in some sort of conflict doesn't mean you aren't allowed to care about your opponent. If you can't muster up the energy to care about the person, then perhaps you should work on developing a care for the subject matter at hand.

If you're in negotiations and they're trying to explain to you why they can't pay, you should care about the predicament enough to listen to their explanations. Active listening doesn't require you to agree with your opponent, it just requires you to listen.

Attention:

This can be a tough one. The mind is extremely busy and might end up wandering in the middle of a sentence. If someone's going on and on, they might end up losing your attention. You may begin to fantasize, remember something or just think about something else entirely. While you lose your focus on the person's words, you aren't fully present. And if you're not fully present in the conversation, important information could slip past you. You might end up being asked a question that you had no clue what they wanted or worse, you could potentially miss out on an important clue that would give you greater insight into how your opponent is currently thinking. You must pay attention and stay present throughout the discussion, even if you find it to be incredibly boring or you were just reminded of something funny.

Observation:

Another piece to active listening is be able to observe your opponent. How are they carrying themselves? What is their facial expression like? Do you see tears in their eyes or are they angry? Are they breathing heavily, are they scared? If you aren't paying attention to the physical actions and gestures that your opponent is taking, then you won't be able to fully understand what is going on.

Body language is one of the most crucial elements to understanding another person's position. Tight, closed off body language can be signs of protectiveness and worry, while loose and open body language can indicate that they are somewhat more friendly. Believe it or not, but the majority of communication is nonverbal, which means that two things are happening in any kind of discussion. First off, words are being used to convey meaning, but there are also nonverbal cues that convey an even deeper meaning. Someone who fidgets and is nervous is more likely to betray the fact that they are uncertain. Someone who keeps eye contact firmly when speaking is relatively confident in what they are saying. The more you are able to observe a person's actions in conjunction with their words, the more understanding you will have of them. Someone who's giving you a sob story with an arched back, puffed out chest and calm voice probably doesn't even believe their own tale. Someone who's trying to stay calm and keep eye contact but has to look away ever few moments might be ashamed. This gives you clues into understanding what is happening within a person. So, pay attention to the way your opponent carries himself.

Active listening, at its core, is the art of being able to fully be present in the conversation and understand what your opponent's position is. If you aren't able to actively listen to the words being said, you don't have all of the necessary information that will allow for you to be able to turn the tables on them. Don't wait for your turn to speak, you have all the time in the world during a discussion. Tuning them out is a quick recipe for disaster. Listen to each and every word said with intent and you will have the upper hand.

Chapter 3: The Human Heart

Now that we've covered the basics of listening, we must now turn our eyes to what is the underlying psychological factor in any person. We humans love to believe that we are rational creatures at our core. We believe that we are intelligent, smart beings that are able to separate our emotions from our decisions. Yet, this couldn't be further from the truth. The reality is that we, as human beings, are primarily governed by our emotions and feelings. While we might want to think that cold, hard reason is in the captain's chair, if you spent any amount of time considering your own past, you might find that is not true. When was the last time you made a stupid decision based on your feelings at the moment? When was the last time a fear or sadness stopped you from doing something that you wanted to do?

There is no shame in admitting that we are emotional creatures. It's just a reality. Yet the principles of negotiation, discussion and outmaneuvering your opponent are often found to be based on the idea that humans are primarily rational beings. This means that all you would need to do is build the best logical case in order to be able to win. Yet, when the logical argument is presented to another person, that person might not even acknowledge the argument due to their emotional state. If we assume that people are widely rational, then we wouldn't need to learn how to listen and discern their emotions, we would just need to learn how to present the best possible facts in the situation.

Believe it or not, but facts rarely win people over. Look in politics, when was the last time a fact was ever capable of changing someone's mind? Both sides that vehemently oppose each other both bring their own facts to the table and claim truth. They both will loudly shout "why won't you listen to reason?" as if reason and fact was responsible for someone's political opinion. The reality is, deep down, people respond more to emotion than they do fact. A politician that is able to make a person feel great, safe, strong, hopeful, happy, excited will be able to influence someone far better than a politician who rolled out a list of facts, *even if those facts are true!* Why is this? Because we as people make decisions based off how we feel. It's part of our general makeup and no matter how smart a person is, or how convinced they are of their own rational superiority, they are making decisions based off of emotions as well.

The problem lies in the idea that rationality is somehow superior to emotion. Rationalism is important, don't get me wrong, but being rational isn't particularly superior to emotion. Neither is emotion superior to rationality. The reality is that they are designed to coexist within a human mind. Yet, we often see these areas at odds. An emotional person is often seen as irrational, whereas a smart person is usually seen as emotionless or in control of their feelings. Yet, when we look at the decision-making process of most individuals, we see that they are often putting their emotions first. Why is that? Because these people often have a low emotional intelligence score.

Just like we have the idea of Intelligence Quotient, or IQ, to measure our ability to think, identify patterns and use our reasoning skills, so do we have an Emotional Quotient. We call this Emotional Intelligence, or EQ. Emotional Intelligence is essentially the way we measure an understanding of our own emotions and the emotions of others. A highly emotional person who can't maintain their composure and a man who claims he has no emotion may actually have the exact same kind of Emotional Intelligence level, it just manifests themselves in different ways. This is groundbreaking when it comes to understanding other people. You see, if we cannot change people's minds so easily by appealing to their intelligence or IQ, then we must realize that we can appeal to others through their sense of emotional intelligence.

What does this mean in terms of practicality? What it means is that since people are primarily governed by their emotions and since most decision making is based on responses to emotions, the greater understanding of emotion that we have, the more persuasive we can become. Here's an interesting question: how do you outmaneuver someone who's crying hysterically about a situation you're involved in? A greater understanding of emotions can enable you to learn just why a person reacts the way that they do. When you understand that, you can learn how to handle them in a discussion much easier. This makes conflict resolution significantly easier than trying to use facts to win. Facts don't win arguments or conflicts. While that might seem somewhat frustrating because it doesn't line up with the modern way of thought (argue your opponent into the ground! Blind them with facts and science!) try to focus on the fact that there is a far better way to win conflicts.

The best way to win a conflict is to identify the emotional state that your opponent is in and learn how you can interact with that emotional state to the best of your ability. The goal isn't to overwhelm them with smart phrases or clever facts, the goal is to actually get your opponent to agree with you. People don't agree with others unless they feel safe enough to do so.

So, let's spend some time talking about the emotional process that occurs within a person once they begin to experience some form of conflict. First off, we must ask ourselves, what triggers a conflict? In most cases, it's a simple case of someone wanting something that the other person doesn't. For example, in argument with your boss who wants you to work overtime, your boss wants you to work and you don't. This is a conflict. If the entire conflict could be settled with pure reason and facts, all you would have to do is give your boss the bullet points as to why you can't work overtime and he would agree with you after reviewing the authenticity of each statement. Does it work like that in real life? Not at all. Usually what happens is that emotions tend to flare on both sides and reason goes right out of the window.

So, we must recognize that the nature of conflict escalates emotion, and it usually escalates the stronger emotions. It rises feelings of fear, anger, disgust, rage or even sorrow. All of these emotions then lead to an exaggerated state of mind, heavily influenced by the feelings. This makes decision making far more of a response to emotion than anything else. In order to understand the person, we must understand the feelings themselves first. Because if you don't understand your own feelings or the feelings inside another human being, then you don't have all the information that you need. Now, there are a wide variety of emotions that are in existence, but in reality, there are only six basic emotions that exist. Every other emotion can be broken down into a category of these six. If we're wanting to learn how to outsmart, outmaneuver and outfox our opponents, then we must be able to understand the role of each of these emotions not only in our opponents, but also in ourselves. Remember, you are no more rational than your opponent, because you are a human too. So, let's look at and discuss each emotion in detail:

Anger:

Anger is one of the strongest primary emotions that exists. The effects on anger on the human body are usually easy to identify. There is an increase of heartrate, blood begins pumping through the body, muscle tension occurs and oxygen intake increases. Feelings of aggression and physical violence can also occur if a person is too angry. Anger can be slow burning or it can be explosive, leading to serious rage issues in a person's life. If you were to ask just about anyone if anger were a bad thing, most people would say yes. But there's a problem, we were created to experience anger for some purpose, weren't we? Is it some random bad emotion that happens within us that we have no control over? One of the biggest problems that modern thought has developed is the idea that emotions themselves are positive or negative. An emotion is actually neutral. They aren't good. They aren't bad. They just are. What they lead us to do can determine if an emotion is good or bad, but the reality is the experience of having an emotion isn't a bad thing.

Yet, what happens when we experience an emotion that we don't regard as pleasant? We can be very quick to classify those things as bad. So, when we see a little kid get angry, we tell them not to get mad, punishing them for the anger. We don't teach them that it's okay for them to be angry, we teach that it's wrong to feel such emotions. The reality is that all emotions, including anger, can be expressed healthily but we are often convinced by our own negative experiences with anger that it is a bad thing.

We must ask ourselves, what is the purpose of anger? Is it just to get you in a state of tension? No! Anger is actually designed to protect you from harm! You see, when a person is under a state of danger, without anger, there would be no desire to act. Imagine, for a moment, that someone is trying to stab you with a knife. A variety of emotions are going to surge through you, fear, worry, surprise, but the strongest emotion at the time will most likely be anger. That anger will motivate you to fight back if you're cornered or unable to escape. In fact, many people who have been in life or death situations with an aggressor have reported that one of the emotions they experienced was anger. Anger is designed to protect you from harm. And that is a good thing, because all of the physiological effects that anger has on the human body is designed to become physically aggressive and protective.

In a conflict where anger is present, we must consider why that anger exists. Why does anger, a self-defensive emotion, rise up when a person is in conflict. Usually, it's because a person is feeling threatened. They are feeling, on some level, that they are under attack and will respond with the full force of their anger. So, when tensions arise, it's because a person is actually feeling under fire. This is why you see big aggressive guys screaming and yelling at their tiny wives or girlfriends. In their minds, even though she has no chance of being able to physically hurt him, something she said has caused him to feel threatened and the anger is a defensive reaction to defend himself from her. It doesn't make much sense on a rational level, but it makes perfect sense on an emotional level.

So, what do we do when we're dealing with an angry person or when we are dealing with anger ourselves? Well, we must first recognize that the emotion is being triggered by some kind of reaction. Something is making them feel threatened and is causing them to respond this way. You don't have to respond back to them the same way. See, what happens when anger in one person rises, it begins to threaten the other person and pretty soon, both parties are angry. But what do you do if you recognize the anger is present due to a person feeling threatened? Do you get just as angry or do you stop to acknowledge that the person is actually in a lower position due to their emotional state? Once you are able to realize that anger is not an offensive emotion, but a *defensive* one, it should drastically change the way you approach the situation. Patience and calmness should prevail within you and you should take steps to address the anger that is happening in front of you. But we'll talk more about tactics in the next chapter.

Fear:

Another emotion in the self-preservation bucket, fear is designed to protect you from trouble. Instead of increasing aggression and violence, fear usually has the effect of causing us to withdraw from the problem. There are healthy fears and there are unhealthy ones. Fear of snakes are healthy, fear of stop signs are unhealthy. The difference? A snake can bite you and hurt you, a stop sign doesn't have any kind of negative effect on your life. Fear is useful and healthy when it comes to self-preservation, but in our modern culture, fear is often seen as one of the worst possible things that can happen emotionally. Whereas older cultures used to deal with fear on a continual basis, our culture is more saturated in things designed to take away fear. Anxiety replaces fear and we find ourselves living lives where we do everything in our power to avoid fear.

What this means is that when a person feels afraid, they can shut down or try to avoid the situation. How can you win an argument or conflict if your opponent retreats, or worse, refuses to talk about the problem? Fear can also have the nasty side effect of provoking anger. Fear is kind of like Anger's little brother, if he's in trouble, anger can show up quickly to protect him. So, someone who's nasty, mean and belligerent might actually be very afraid. The two emotions often intermingle together.

The best way to combat fear is to simply acknowledge that it exists. Fear can't be rationalized away, it can't be wished away and no facts will remove the fear. Instead, fear can simply be walked through. When we see that a conflict is rooted in fear, we must then make the decision to do what we can to help our opponent feel safe. The safer your opponent feels, the better chance you have of influencing them properly.

Disgust:

Disgust is a selective emotion. It essentially allows for us to sort between things that are pleasant and unpleasant, healthy and unhealthy, good or bad. For example, someone eating a rotten apple will react with the emotion of disgust, which will lead the individual to throwing the apple out rather than to continue munching away. Disgust also occurs on ethical and moral grounds as well, for example, if someone hears about a murderer, they might react to the news with disgust, having their sense of morality offended.

Disgust within a conflict exists purely as a reaction to ideas presented. When a person sees disgust, they tend to react with their own level of adverse reaction. For example, if a conflict arises between two friends about where they want to eat and the first man reacts to the second man's suggestion with disgust, it can elicit disgust in the second man as well and now they are at odds. It's helpful and healthy to make a point to try and mask your own disgust reaction, or at least make a point to clearly communicate why you disapprove of a situation without making the other person feel that they themselves are disgusting.

Sadness:

Sadness is certainly one of the more familiar emotions that exists within us. Everyone has, at some point, been sad and feeling low about something. Sadness is usually caused by some kind of external event, such as loss, pain or devastation. In general, sadness is just a way for us to process emotional pain, and while we don't particularly like the way it feels, we must accept that it is just a fact of life. There will be times when you feel sad and there will be times when you feel happy.

How does sadness affect us when it comes to negotiation and conflict resolution? Well truthfully it can be hard to tell, as sadness is one of the more hidden emotions in people. Those who are weeping during a conflict are usually feeling either fear or disgust(shame) not sadness. Those who truly are feeling sadness shouldn't be hounded or pushed, because sorrow creates a vulnerable person.

Surprise:

Surprise is indeed an emotion, it's caused by something catching you off unaware of the situation at hand. They can be pleasant or unpleasant. A man getting a surprise birthday party is a very pleasant experience, whereas on the other hand receiving a surprised paternity lawsuit can be very unpleasant.

It's extremely important to gauge whether surprise is present within a person's mind when you begin to resolve conflict between the two of you. If a person feels surprised with something unpleasant, they can quickly grow defensive or frustrated. On the other hand, if they are prepared for some kind of conflict, it might be easier to navigate through the problem at hand, rather than just get involved in a serious fight that goes nowhere.

You should be prepared for the emotional response that you have when you are surprised as well. Many times, you can experience an influx of emotion when you feel surprised by something and you might have the knee-jerk reaction to get into a fight when you don't need to be on the offensive, just because you are surprised. By learning to identify how you react when you feel surprised by something unpleasant, you are better preparing yourself for dealing with problems in the future.

Happiness:

The final emotion on the list of primary emotions is happiness. The emotion is almost always regarded as pleasant and is the ideal emotion that you want to produce not only in yourself, but also in your opponent. When your opponent is happy, they are more inclined to agree with your desires, they are more friendly and best of all, you have a better chance of your relationship growing stronger together.

These emotions are all part of the human equation. When you understand these emotions and how they work, you have a greater chance of being able to work with people and resolve conflict in your own favor. Humans are emotional beings and will almost always make decisions in favor of how their emotions are affecting them at the time, meaning that the best possible way you can learn how to overcome conflict is to focus on learning as much as you can about how emotions affect yourself and other people. With that in mind, let's go ahead and head to the next and final section about tactics that will help you outmaneuver your foes.

Chapter 4: How to Win

Alright, so now we're at the part of the book where we are going to start putting theory into application. So, we've spent time already looking at how to listen and understand your opponent, we've looked into how emotion primarily influences a human far more than facts do and we've seen the different emotions that can affect a discussion. Now we've got to put all of this head knowledge into application. We're going to do this first by breaking down the anatomy of a conflict into a few key parts.

Conflict Component 1: Desire

All conflict can be summed up as this: I desire blank, but you stand in the way somehow. In negotiation, it could be as simple as, I desire to buy this car for 10,000 dollars, but you (the salesman) stand in the way. It could be very abstract, such as I desire peace and safety, but you (my husband) are preventing me from having that.

Since all conflict can be summed up as desire pushing against desire, it then comes to the point where we must readily acknowledge that there can be winners and losers in these kinds of fights. Usually, we look at winning as a zero-sum game, meaning that if you win, it's at the expense of the other person. Hopefully by this point you should know that the reality is that true victory is when all parties are satisfied with a conflict, because that is the only way for a conflict to reach true resolution.

Conflict Component 2: Threat

The second component to conflict is the feeling of a threat existing. This comes from a sense that one's desire is under some kind of assault. This is where the tension and emotional danger comes into play. For example, if you desire to take a day off and your boss wants you to stay and work on Saturday, there is a natural feeling of a threat existing. What threatens you is that you can potentially lose out on a day of enjoying yourself and resting, what threatens your boss is that he could potentially lose out on getting important things done.

The threat game then leads to escalation. Please note that when I am saying threat, I'm not saying that your boss is threatening you, such as a death threat or saying he will fire you, what I mean by threat is that it signals some kind of potential loss and that loss is seen as a bad thing. This is what causes emotions to increase, is the sense of threat. Once both parties feel threatened about something, the conflict continues to escalate.

Conflict Component 3: Ego

Once threat arrives, we must then deal with our own inflated sense of self. It should come as no surprise to you that most people are relatively self-focused and some are even narcissistic. This is the ego and essentially it is the biggest reason why we have some painful conflicts in our lives. Trying to negotiate with a boss with a colossal ego is hard, convincing a narcissistic person to see things your way is extremely hard.

The ego, more or less, is the biggest problem in conflict resolution because it stands in the way of reaching a consensus. When you get a big ego and a sense of being threatened you get even more trouble than you probably wanted. You get an extremely emotional person trying to protect themselves.

Conflict Component 4: Self-Protection

The reality is that people are fiercely protective of their own selves. They don't want to be taken advantage of, they don't want to be worked over, bullied, beaten up or otherwise be a loser in any kind of situation. When a person feels they are under attack, they will attack back out of a sense of desire to protect the self. This is the part where extreme emotions such as anger, fear or sadness can arrive. The ego is typically fairly sensitive and since it can't bear the thought of experiencing pain, or being treated poorly, it will use self-protection to try and stop whatever is happening.

So, as you can see, from these four elements combined together, it essentially turns a conflict into a seriously windy maze that you'll need to navigate through in order to reach victory. Think of it as learning how to navigate, rather than learning how to overcome. You see, people are not obstacles. They are important and valuable human beings with hopes, dreams and ideas of their own. If you view them as a problem, then you run the risk of not being able to truly get them to see your way of thinking. If you view the conflict as the obstacle, it's a far better perspective to have. Don't focus on defeating your opponent, focus on achieving your goals. It's an entirely different way of thinking.

So how do you outmaneuver them and get what you really want? Well, let's look at the elements of victory.

Victory Element 1: Goal

The most important part of figuring out what kind of victory that you want in a conflict is to determine just exactly what your goals are. Do you want to get an agreement out of someone? Do you want to prevent someone from inflicting their will upon you? Do you want to get them to see things through your point of view? Any of these goals are perfectly fine to aspire towards, but it's important you do indeed have at least one goal. It's no good trying to reach conflict resolution without having some ideal ending in mind. You've got to be willing to work toward some goal and keep that goal in mind as you deal with the conflict.

Victory Element 2: Cooperation

Another element of victory is learning how to cooperate with your opponent. This doesn't mean that you have to agree with his position or demands, but what it does mean is that you are going to need to learn how to get along with him, so that as you are working your way towards reaching your own goals, you aren't tripped up by causing more intense interpersonal conflicts. In other words, a spirit of cooperation is what will allow you to separate your ego from the conflict.

Taking things personally can be one of the worst possible decisions that you can make as you try to reach resolution. The only way to avoid taking things personally is to have a cooperative attitude from the beginning. By making the conscious decision to be on both sides, to be fair and to work to help your opponent out, you are reducing the chances of you taking something personally.

So why not take things personally? Quite simply, when you take things personally, your emotions will begin to elevate as well. If you are in a conflict with a friend and they, in anger, throw out something hurtful, if you take it personally, you will begin to reach a compromising state of emotional frustration yourself, leading you to take actions that could be potentially destructive. Don't forget, we are emotional creatures and we do not make the most rational decisions when our emotions are going unchecked. The best way for you to resist taking things personally is to have your opponent's best interest in mind.

Victory Element 3: Being Calm

One of the most important things that you must bring to the table in conflict is the ability to stay resilient and strong. You must be able to resist The Pull, you must be able to keep your emotions in check and you must, above all, make sure to never rush. Just because your opponent is throwing some fast facts at you, or has accused you of something that is a lie, doesn't mean that you have to react according to how they want you to react. Instead, keep calm and focus on what you want to do. Being defensive will only trip you up. The reality is, the more relaxed and calm you are, the better chances you have of winning the discussion or argument. The moment you begin to rush, get flustered or try to argue against false charges, without thinking is the moment that you begin to lose your position. Stay centered and ready to discuss things without heat or anger.

Most people aren't expecting a calm response or softness. They are usually expecting some kind of heated blowout, or pushback. By learning how to slow down and respond thoughtfully and carefully to their words, you will literally take them by surprise and improve your position. Most people, when heated, will run out of steam after some time, so by learning how to keep your cool, even in the face of someone who is treating you with contempt, malice or rage, you are actually diffusing their only source of power. This will force them to slow down and eventually reach a point where emotion isn't primarily the thing driving them forward. Instead, they will be able to reach a place where they might even be willing to listen to your words and consider them.

So, those are the elements of conflict and victory. Now, we're going to start discussing some tried and true tactics that can be used in any kind of argument or discussion that will improve your ability to outmaneuver your opponent and get what you really want. These tactics, when used in conjunction with all of the other things you've learned from this book, will put you over the top when it comes to solving conflicts with ease and skill. But be warned, don't think that you can just rely on some cheap tricks in order to win. You must firmly apply all of the other principles in this book if you want to achieve greatness. As the saying goes, a man convinced against his will is of the same opinion still. Don't fall into the trap of thinking that you can use persuasion as some kind of Jedi mind trick, to sucker people into doing your bidding. Let's get started.

Tactic 1: Mirroring

Mirroring is one of the oldest tactics in the book. When it comes down to it, body language plays a huge role in how we are received and how people receive us. When we are trying to become more influential when talking to others, we can use the power of body language to get them to perceive us more favorably. This is done through the tactic known as mirroring. The art of mirroring involves basically matching your opponent's body position physically. So, if they are standing there, one foot forward, arm at their side and hand on the chin, by slowly and subtly adopting that same stance, it will cause them to subconsciously consider you as more of a friend. Why? It's primarily because we like people who are similar to us and those who are standing like us or imitating us give us a sense of worth and accomplishment.

Mirroring is exceptionally useful, but you need to be careful that you don't do it so dramatically that it looks like you are trying to purposefully mock them. By matching their tone, body language and expression, you will be able to get your message to them better.

Tactic 2: Power of Touch

Touching a person on the shoulder, or elbow can actually go a long way when it comes to navigating through conflict. If the person is someone you are in a romantic relationship with, prolonged physical contact can increase the feeling of safety between you and your opponent. This will allow for them to feel a little calmer and allow you both to empathize with one another more easily. The reason why touch is so powerful is because we are designed to respond to physical touch, it releases a bevy of hormones that cause positive feelings and bonding. Of course, it's important to make sure that your touch is organic and gentle, not forceful, violent or done in any way that could be construed as aggression. Usually touch works later on in the discussion, when both parties have started to calm down.

Tactic 3: Eye Contact (But not Too much)

Occasional eye contact can help during a conflict, as long as it is not an intense and violent gaze. If you are calm and gentle with your glances, if you let your eyes linger for a few minutes as you speak, you will increase the sense of connection between you and your opponent. This can help them feel more at ease and will hopefully decrease the amount of intensity between you two. Don't keep eye contact prolonged but make sure you aren't avoiding looking directly at them. Refusal to look at a person during a conflict is usually construed as cowardice and may give your opponent the feeling that they are winning the conflict, causing them to get a boost in their ego.

Tactic 4: Acknowledgement

As you're working with a person, even if they are incredibly wrong about whatever it is they are saying, you must be willing to acknowledge what they said without dismissing them. It is incredibly easy to dismiss someone's words, especially when we feel they are incorrect, but when you dismiss someone's words, they will feel like you are dismissing them as a person. By making the conscious decision to acknowledge what they are saying, to repeat what they said or ask clarifying questions so you can better understand them, you will be able to help them get a sense that you genuinely care about their position. This will allow them in turn to lower their guard and then you can address the problem with their words. If you try to defeat the argument without acknowledging them, it will only serve to make them more defensive.

Tactic 5: Clarify

One major method of navigating through a disagreement is to clarified your opponent's position is. You can ask follow-up questions to understand their statements better, you can ask them what they mean, you can even go as far as to ask them what their goal is, but the most important thing is to make sure that you fully explore their position before you try and shape the agenda. By asking clarifying questions, you will be able to get a better sense of where they are. Think of it like exploration, the more you explore, the more you know what you're up against. The less you explore, the bigger chance you have of losing.

Tactic 6: Repeat

If you're not able to understand what your opponent is saying, or you need more information but don't know exactly what to ask him, then here's a clever little tactic that you can use, it will work just about every time you do it. All you need to do is take the last few words of their sentence and repeat it back, except repeat it like a question. For example, if you were arguing with someone who said "You never listen to me and it makes me angry!" You could simply say "It makes you angry?" This will then trigger them to actually expound on the situation. This is a great way to keep someone talking as a way to gain more information or to better understand the scenario. If you're trying to figure out what to say next, this could even give you more time. Just repeat the last few words they said as a question and it will get them going. Most of the time people won't even notice. This is most likely due to the fact that the biggest thing just about everyone on this planet truly wants is to be understood. So, giving people an opportunity to be better understood will often spur them on to continue giving you more information.

Tactic 7: Avoid judging statements

It's extremely important that as you navigate your way through a conflict that you don't use judging statements. A judging statement is simply one where you make a declaration that essentially guesses what the person's motives are. For example, "you don't care about me" is a judging statement. Saying "when you don't take out the trash, I don't feel cared about" is a much better way to state your feelings. A judging statement doesn't do anything except cause more defensiveness in a person. But by stating how you feel in the conflict, by making the discussion more of a reflection on how you feel, you are avoiding the pitfall that most people fall into. You don't really know what's happening in another person's mind, so for you to make judgements about their actions will only cause even more bad blood to happen between you. You'd be far more apt to explain your feelings and emotions when someone conveys how they feel about your actions, than if they conveyed what your motivations were.

Tactic 8: State Your Emotions

An important thing to do when dealing with serious conflict is to make sure that you are able to properly convey how you feel during the conversation. By acknowledging your own emotions, you are able to take greater control of your own self as well as help break the ice in the conversation. Most people lose sight of their opponent's feelings during a conflict, so by you making the decision to state how you feel, it can help humanize you to your opponent. Once again, avoid accusations, such as "you are making me angry!" instead try to focus on saying things like "I'm feeling angry right now." This is a healthier way to express your emotions and it takes the edge out of your feelings. The more you acknowledge your emotions, the less intense that they will feel within you. This is an excellent way to maintain your composure, which will allow you to dance circles around an opponent who is less capable of controlling their own emotions.

Tactic 9: Find Common Ground

One thing that you absolutely need to do if you want your opponent to agree with you on the big goal is to work towards getting them to agree with you on a series of small agreements. Each time that you get your opponent to agree with you on something, it increases the amount of cooperation between you two. It allows you both to feel a little more connected and if you pull this off just right, you can get them to eventually agree to whatever your major goal is.

Tactic 10: Be Willing to Compromise

No one wants to lose in a conflict. The best kinds of victories are the ones in which both parties receive what they want to some degree. If you're going to be engaging in conflict or a negotiation, you must be willing to compromise on some level. Now, the goal is always to get your way, but it's important to balance yourself between rampant idealism and being realistic. It can be hard to get your way all the time, so by making the decision to be willing to compromise, you are enhancing your chances of success in the conflict even more. A compromise might not always be possible, but the reality is that the reason most conflicts and negotiations fail is because people are unable to check their egos at the door. A compromise is the antidote to a serious conflict because it allows for both parties to reach some level of agreement, even if it's not fully what you wanted. It is better to receive half than to receive nothing at all. Leave your ego at the door and be willing to work with them. In the long run, this will benefit your relationship far more than if you just browbeat them into agreeing with you.

Conclusion

Ultimately, navigating conflict, overcoming challenges and learning how to push past the natural defenses that people put up can be some of the most rewarding things that you can ever do with your life. Remember, the goal of a good conflict isn't to crush your opponent, because that only will push against them, making them resist you even more. The goal is to be like water, flexible and free, flowing back and forth, gently pushing and moving around them, in the hopes of getting them to see things through your point of view. The more you are able to understand your opponents, the more insight that you can have into their emotional state, the more you will be able to win these conflicts without a problem.

Never forget that the reality of life is that humans are very emotional creatures. They don't always act as rationally as they believe they do and their feelings can lead them to make decisions that go against their best interest. By learning to control your own emotions, understand their emotions and learning how to navigate around them in such a way to get them to see your point of view as good for them, you will be able to outsmart, outmaneuver and outfox any person in your way!

—

Made in the USA
Lexington, KY
26 May 2019